My Cuban
COCKTAIL
RECIPE BOOK

My Cuban

COCKTAIL

RECIPE BOOK

Ramón Pedreira Rodríguez

EDITORIAL ARTE Y LITERATURA

Original title in Spanish: *Mi recetario de cocteles cubanos*
Translated by: Carmen González
Edited by: Dania Pérez Rubio and Fernando Nápoles Tapia
Cover photograph by: Julio Larramendi
Cover design by: Julio Antonio Mompeller
Photographs by: Julio Larramendi and Havana Club International S. A.
Electronics composition by: Beatriz Roussó
Printed in: Editorial Linotipia Bolívar y Cía. S. en C.
Bogotá, D. C. - Colombia

We acknowledge our gratitude for the cooperation given by Havana Club International S. A. in providing several of the photographs included in this volume.

Second English-language edition: 2000
Thirt English-language edition: 2004

© 1997, Ramón Pedreira Rodríguez
© 1997, Editorial Arte y Literatura

ISBN 959-03-0073-1

EDITORIAL ARTE Y LITERATURA
Instituto Cubano del Libro
Calle O' Reilly No. 4, esq. a Tacón
La Habana Vieja, CP 10 100, La Habana, Cuba

Contents

Preface

A thousand? Five thousand? Ten thousand? No one really knows how many recipes are used worldwide nowadays to mix a good cocktail.

To prepare any of these wonderful recipes, all known alcoholic and non-alcoholic beverages can be mixed in adequate proportions with various brews, fruits, milk, egg and honey, and flavored with herbs and other aromatic ingredients.

Successful cocktails are human creations that can travel far and wide in time and space, like Martinis and Manhattans, whose recipes have remained unchanged for more than one hundred years. Daiquiris, Cuba Libres, Tom Collins and Sangarees are mixed today in exactly the same way they were prepared some seventy-odd years ago, and they are still included in the price lists of famous bars and restaurants.

Cocktails are the most popular drinks in developed societies. It is not by chance that they are served in the best bars. Although cocktails were first created as before-meal drinks, currently there are cocktails for every occasion: apéritifs, digestive, refreshing, betweentimes, nourishing, hot, etc.

Cocktails can be very simple or quite complex and fanciful, according to how they are prepared. In regard to flavor, they range from extra-dry to sweet, from very strong to light. Cocktails can also be served cold, hot or at room temperature, to suit every taste. Even concoctions prepared for sick people, teetotallers and children are called cocktails.

Cocktails are named after their creators, geographical regions, memorable dates, places where they are served, famous people. To have a cocktail not only means to enjoy new tastes and aromas other than the ones of alcohol, but also to take nourishment that pure drinks lack, which renders them healthier and more nutritious.

The cocktail recipes included in this book were chosen from among the best created in Cuba.

Some are hallmarks of the premises where they are served; others have won competitions held every year in various Cuban cities; several have remained on the price lists for years; but they are all fine combinations in which the exquisite Cuban rum is always present.

We are sure they will satisfy the most demanding gourmets.

Enjoy them!

THE AUTHOR

THE ORIGIN OF COCKTAILS

CUBA COCKTAIL

In a large cocktail shaker, mix: tropical sun, fine sand, a crystal clear sea and human warmth. Serve it in a Caribbean island shaped like a crocodile. Sprinkle lavishly with happiness and garnish it with luxuriant vegetation.

Although people have been mixing drinks for many years, and adding fruit and other products, and seasoning them with spice, cocktails as they are known today had their origin in the United States by the end of the 18th century. Then they were taken abroad to other countries where American presence and influence were strong. There is no doubt that artificially produced ice had a vital importance in the development of cocktails.

When then National Prohibition Act was passed by Congress in 1919[1], cocktails were already an American institution and hundreds of recipes were prepared every day in thousands of bars all over the nation. In 1933, the Prohibition was repealed and sales of intoxicating liquors were authorized.

This fourteen-year period had a strong impact on Cuba. Local distilleries in association with American smugglers exported large amounts of rum to the United States and thousands of thirsty tourists invaded the countless bars that opened in Havana. Never before had this city known of so many bartenders nor so many wonderful new cocktail recipes were created and served.

1. The National Prohibition Act or Volstead Act was passed by Congress on October, 1919 and made effective in 1920, as the XVIII Amendment to the Constitution. It was repealed by the XXIII Amendment voted by Congress on February, 1933. —Ed.

THE ORIGIN OF THE WORD COCKTAIL

There are countless versions and speculations about the origin of the word cocktail, spelled *coctel* in Spanish. But it is still not known where and when the name was used for the first time.

The word cocktail is formed by the words cock and tail. Therefore, it can be surmised that it originated from the compounding of these two terms. One of the versions about how it was applied to mixed drinks, says that the first person to ever mix two beverages, only had cockerel feathers handy to stir the mixture.

Another version says it was named after the daughter of a Mexican indigenous chief, and later adopted by the North Americans.

In his book *La Bebida* (Liquor, 1935), Ullivarry tells the amusing story of Giovanni Angelo Martini, an Italian-American who, in 1785, opened a barge service to transport goods on the banks of the Potomac river. Every year for Christmas, Giovanni's uncle Maturino sent him vermouth from Italy, while his first cousin Pasquale Calcavecchia Lewis, an engineer who lived in Havana, sent him Cuban rum.

Giovanni never lacked gin, which he got from the loads his barges carried to Philadelphia, Newark, New York and Boston.

As usual, in 1785 Giovanni invited his friends and neighbors to celebrate Christmas in his home. But this time he had a surprise for them. After thinking and experimenting for months, the apéritifs he served were various mixtures chilled in a dry hog bladder, filled with snow from the Potomac.

He called cocktails this calculated mixture of beverages, for they had the colors of the tails of fighting cocks from Jerez de la Frontera, in Spain.

He named the first mixture Martini after himself and the second, Havana Club, like the rum his cousin the *habanero* Calcavecchia sent him from Cuba. He named the third one after an Englishman who wore a dark hat and whose name Martini never knew. That gentleman had presented him with two barrels of good rye whiskey. However, as Giovanni did not yet master the English language, he placed adjectives after nouns like it is done in Italian. Therefore, the original name: Man's Hat Tan, became Manhattan.

James Fenimore Cooper presents a more serious version about the origin of cocktails in his series *Leatherstocking Tales*, a collection of five famous novels. Cooper wrote that Betsy Flanagan, a young Irishwoman who owned a tavern near New York around the year 1779 was the reason this name was used for the first time.

Her tavern was the meeting place for American and French officers in George Washington's army, who wanted to relax when they were off duty and drink an alcoholic combination that allegedly granted courage and strength. The officers used to tease Betsy by comparing the chickens she served with the beautiful ones that belonged to one of her neighbors, said to be a Tory (North Americans who supported Great Britain during the War of Independence). So, Betsy decided to play a mean trick on them.

No true patriot bought anything from a Tory. So Betsy purchased the chickens from her neighbor and made a feast for her clients. When they finished eating, they went to the bar for a drink of their favorite alcoholic beverage.

To their amazement, they found that each one of the bottles of their usual drinks was decorated with a single feather of the tails of the cockerels from the Tory's coop. Some of the officers were annoyed by the tavernkeeper's practical joke, but suddenly one of the French officers, to break the ice, proposed the following toast: "Long live the cock's tail!" And from then on, Betsy's combinations were thus known.

According to the 1938 edition of *Larousse's Gastronomical Dictionary*, the name cocktail might be derived either from the similarity of the colors of the cockerel tail's feathers, and those of the various liquors used in the mixture, or after the name of a highly seasoned brew prepared by Manhattan's first settlers to incite themselves to drink. They stirred that brew with long feathers plucked from cockerels' tails.

Some authors say the word cocktail was derived from the French *coquetel*, used in Bordeaux in the late 18th century as a name for mixed beverages.

But whether it was first used in one place or another, cocktail is the name currently given to the mixture of alcoholic beverages to which fruit juices, soft drinks, milk, eggs and other ingredients are added. Fruit, shellfish and fish—the two latter ones accompanied with cold sauces—, cut into little portions and served as entreés before the main course, are also called cocktails.

Cubans have given countless names to the mixture of alcoholic beverages, like *meneo, meneíto, revuelto, batido, compuesto, sambumbia, ponche, chiringuito,* etc.

Places That Served Alcoholic Beverages in Cuba

The first places on the largest of the West Indies to serve alcoholic beverages, served wine from Spain and afterward also *aguardiente*, strong spirits. They were generically called *botillerías*—liquor and wineshops—and specifically, wine shops, general stores, taverns and inns. Meals were also served in some of these places, like the taverns, while inns also took lodgers.

Some time later, hostels and taverns began offering a wider variety of drinks.

The owners of many of these public houses plied their trade in their own homes; therefore, their houses were furnished with large, rustic tables and wooden benches or rustic chairs upholstered with untanned cattle hide. Barrels stored in the corners were generally used sometimes, according to their size, as tables and chairs.

In time, taverns mushroomed. Typical taverns had a counter where customers stood enjoying their drinks.

The military and their garrisons multiplied during the wars of independence. Saloons—called *cantinas* in Spanish—became the fashion then. They were usually placed near the garrisons, where soldiers and officers could buy beverages and cold meats as well as a variety of personal effects that the quartermaster did not supply.

The term *cantina* took so much root among the Cuban people, that it is still broadly used to name any public house that serves alcoholic and non-alcoholic drinks. Saloon bartenders are called *cantineros* in Spanish.

During the second half of the 19th century, the Spanish word *barra*, derived from the English bar, began to be used to describe a bigger and more modern saloon, with refrigeration and an even wider assortment of alcoholic beverages and soft drinks. Some authors say *barras* were called thus after the shape of their counters; others, however, rightly point out that it was due to the fact that a cylindrical metal bar was clamped to the floor along the counter, at a height of some 15 centimeters, for customers to rest their feet.

The word bar became fashionable in Havana after the North American intervention in the early 1900s. It was used by North Americans who visited or lived in the city, and by the local bourgeoisie, who often travelled to the United States. After that, stools were placed before the counters, and decorations became more lavish.

Rum: An Essential Ingredient for Mixing Cuban Cocktails

Rum has been known in the West Indies since 1650, and has been commercially produced in Cuba for more than a century. It is an alcoholic beverage distilled from fermented sugar cane juice and from the molasses that results from sugar manufacture.

After the juice has been squeezed out of the sugar cane, it is boiled so that part of its water contents evaporates, thus becoming a thick syrup or massecuite. The massecuite is poured into a centrifuge that turns at a rate of two thousand revolutions per minute, purging the molasses and leaving small sugar crystals.

The molasses is sent to distilleries where it is stored in large vats, mixed with water and yeast. This combination is called *batición*, and is stored for fermentation in wooden or iron coolers, for about thirty hours.

During that time, the yeast turns the saccharose into alcohol. When this part of the process is over, distilling begins in order to obtain various types of alcohol, among them, a slightly aromatic, transparent raw rum used to manufacture rums. It is filtered through sand and charcoal, and stored in large oak casks to age from five to seven years. The rums obtained in this process are mixed before being bottled, to attain the standard commercially required quality.

Three types of rum are basically produced: extra aged, old gold and light dry.

Havana Club, Caney, Legendario, Matusalén, Pinilla and Caribbean Club are just a few among the most renowned Cuban rum trademarks. The exceptional quality of Cuban rum is unanimously acknowledged worldwide. According to connoisseurs, it is due, in the first place, to the quality of our sugar cane, the richness of the soil and the island's climate, that yield high-quality molasses to produce Cuban rum, and mainly to the methods of fermentation and distillation used, and to the know-how and responsibility of the technicians who participate in the entire process.

How to Mix Cuban Cocktails

It all depends on what you want to prepare. You may only need a simple glass, ice, a stirrer and the beverages needed for a Cuba Libre, or a more complete set of utensils for a cocktail service and the necessary ingredients to mix, with utmost precision, any cocktail you fancy.

A complete list follows, of what is essentially needed to prepare even the most demanding Cuban cocktails. However, some of these ingredients can be replaced by other more easily available ones.

Bar Utensils

. Mixing glass for stirred cocktails.

. Cocktail shaker. It is a type of double glass. They are made of metal, or metal and glass. Cocktail shakers are the symbol of bartenders all over the world.

. Electric mixer to prepare frappé cocktails like the Daiquiri.

. Juicer.

. Measuring cup. It is a metal or glass vessel used to measure the exact quantities of the beverages in a cocktail.

. Strainer. Three types of strainers are used: conch strainers, spiral strainers and net strainers.

. Openers. There are four different kinds: corkscrews, metal cap openers, can openers and coconut borers.

. Knives.

. Spoons. The typical cocktail spoon has a long, spiral-shaped handle, and is used to stir cocktails. A teaspoon is needed to measure sugar.

. Funnel.

. Containers for fruit preserves.

. Containers for fruit juices.

. Ice bowls.

. Sugar bowls.

. The utensils to manipulate ice are tongs for ice cubes, small shovels for frappé ice and an ice pick with several sharp ends to chip the ice into pieces.

. Tongs to handle fruit slices, sprigs of peppermint and other ingredients used to garnish cocktails.

. Dropper vials filled with beverages used only in small quantities.

. Kitchen cloths. Bartenders use them to polish glasses and utensils, to dry the counter and to dry their hands.

Serving Utensils

The following are needed to serve the Cuban cocktails whose recipes are included in this book:

. 6-ounce, 8-ounce, 12-ounce and 14-ounce glasses.

. Old Fashion glasses.

. 1.5-ounce and 2 ounce glasses.

. Shallow 3-ounce cocktail stemmed glasses.

. Tall cocktail glasses. They have a 5-ounce capacity and are used for cocktails mixed in a cocktail shaker.

. 6-ounce wine glasses.

. Daiquiri glasses, with bells shaped like orange halves. These glasses have 4- to 6-ounce capacity and are used for frappé cocktails.

. Water glasses. Their capacity ranges from 8 to 10 ounces.

· 8-ounce champagne glasses.

Other utensils needed to complete the set for serving Cuban cocktails:

· Coasters.

· Stirrers.

· Paper napkins.

· Straws.

· Toothpicks. Toothpicks are used to garnish some cocktails.

· Small spoons used for cocktails like Mojitos, since some people like to bruise the sprigs of peppermint in the bottom of the glass. Others, use them to crush lemon slices used as garnishing.

Ingredients to Prepare Cuban Cocktails

1. Water and soft drinks (soda water, cola and lemon sodas)

2. Ice

3. Sugar

4. Eggs

5. Milk (fresh milk, evaporated milk and milk cream)

6. Spices (ground cinnamon, ground nutmeg and cloves)

7. Seasonings (table salt, hot sauce and Worcester sauce)

8. Sprigs of peppermint

9. Mints, balm and basil

10. Fruits and vegetables (lemon, oranges, grapefruit, pineapple and cherry)

11. Fruit juices and tomato juice

12. Bitters

Serving Drinks

Many alcoholic beverages were meant to be drunk and sold straight. That is why their manufacturers endowed each of them with a distinctive trait. There may be many similar beverages, but none of them is exactly like the others.

However, mixed drinks became the fashion decades ago, to the extent that they are currently the favorites of most consumers. Thus, there are several ways in which to serve alcoholic beverages:

· Straight

· Highball

· Frappé

· On the rocks

· Cocktails

According to how they are prepared, cocktails can be:

· Hand blent in a cocktail shaker

· Stirred in a mixing glass

· Blent in an electric mixer

· Mixed in the same glass where they are served

Rules on How to Mix Cocktails

Certain rules must be observed when mixing alcoholic beverages among themselves or with other ingredients:

· The first step is to get the glass where the cocktail will be served.

· If a chilled glass is required, fill it with frappé ice or with ice cubes, or keep a supply of glasses ready in the icebox.

· Do not handle the ingredients with bare hands. Use the shovel for the ice, the tongs for the fruit, and other utensils, according to what you are doing.

· Ingredients must be measured using measuring cups in grams, ounces or milliliters, or measuring spoons according to what is being measured.

· Begin by mixing the beverages required by the recipe in smaller quantities.

· If the ingredients include sugar, dissolve it in any other non-alcoholic beverage included in the recipe before adding the spirituous liquor.

· Estimate the number of cocktails you are preparing according to the capacity of the container used to mix the ingredients, so that there is always ample room to prevent spilling the contents. Remember that when a liquid is shaken, it ripples and expands.

· Ice is the last thing to add, just before stirring, shaking or mixing the cocktail. Take care that it is clean.

· In each case, use the required type of ice. If you use cracked or shaved ice in shaken cocktails, the cocktail will become watery. If, on the contrary, you use large cubes for an electrically mixed cocktail, the mixer may be damaged or large pieces of ice will remain in the drink.

• Ingredients in stirred cocktails are blent with a circular motion of the stirrer for approximately ten seconds.

• The shaker must be used swiftly, energetically and rhythmically, for the crux of a successful cocktail is to mix it in as little time as possible so it does not turn watery. The ice must hit the top and the bottom of the shaker for some fifteen seconds.

•After the cocktail is shaken, it is left to rest in the shaker, placed upright on the counter, for five seconds, so it expels part of the air molecules accumulated while it was being shaken.

• Cocktails are mixed in the electric mixer for some fifteen seconds, until all the ingredients are uniformly blent.

• When preparing two or more cocktails at a time, fill half the glasses first and use the rest of the mixture to complete each full measure.

• Pour the cocktail without filling the glasses to the brim, to avoid spilling it.

• Leftovers must not be used in preparing another drink.

• Verify the specific weight of each beverage when you are preparing multicolored pousse-café cocktails that must not blend, so that the densest beverages sink and the lighter ones remain on top. This will prevent blending the colors of different liquors. Follow the order in which the beverages appear in the recipe.

Table of Approximately Equivalent Measures

- 1 ounce = 30 milliliters

  30 grams

a tablespoon filled almost to overflowing

- 0.5 ounces = 15 milliliters

a teaspoon filled almost to overflowing

- 180 grams = a 10-ounce glass filled with ice cubes

- 15 grams = a level teaspoon of sugar

. 120 grams = one Daiquiri glass not completely full of frappé ice

- 90 grams = a 6-ounce glass full of small ice cubes

Remember that one milliliter is equal to one cubic centimeter.

Cuba Libre.

Bar at the Bodeguita del Medio restaurant.

Havana Club rum manufacturing plant at Santa Cruz del Norte.

Oak casks to age rum.

Laboratory at the Santa Cruz del Norte rum manufacturing plant.

Cuban rums.

Cuban fruits.

Mojito.

Bar at the Floridita restaurant.

Daiquirí Rebelde (Rebel Daiquiri).

Havana Especial (Havana Special).

A bartender at work.

Different Cuban cocktails.

Presidente Seco (Dry President).

Daiquirí Frappé.

Very garnished cocktails.

SOME CUBAN COCKTAILS OF ALL TIMES

ALMENDARES

Betweentimes cocktail, mixed in a cocktail shaker.

Serve it in a chilled, tall cocktail glass.

Ingredients: Grenadine, 5 drops; red curaçao, 5 drops; pineapple juice, 1.5 ounce (45 milliliters); light dry rum, 1.5 ounce (45 milliliters); ice cubes, 6 ounces (180 grams).

How to mix it: Pour the ingredients in the shaker and shake for 15 seconds. Strain them directly into the glass.

This cocktail was named after a famous Havana hotel located on the banks of the Almendares river in the 1920s.

ALTA COCINA (HAUTE CUISINE)

Apéritif, stirred in a mixing glass.

Serve it in a chilled, shallow, stemmed cocktail glass.

Ingredients: Coffee liquor, 0.2 ounce (6 milliliters); dry white vermouth, 1 ounce (30 milliliters); old gold rum, 1 ounce (30 milliliters); ice cubes, 6 ounces (180 grams); 1 olive.

How to mix it: Pour the ingredients in the mixing glass and stir for 10 seconds. Place the olive in the serving glass and strain the cocktail directly into it.

Alta Cocina was the school of gastronomy where Cuban technicians were trained in the 1960s. It was located in the premises of the Tropicana nightclub.

ARCO IRIS (RAINBOW)

Digestive cocktail, mixed in the serving glass.

Serve it in a 1.5-ounce tall, cordial glass.

Ingredients: Grenadine or cacao liquor, 0.25 ounce (7 milliliters); maraschino, 0.25 ounce (7 milliliters); green mint liquor, 0.25 ounce (7 milliliters); red curaçao, 0.25 ounce (7 milliliters); yellow chartreuse, 0.25 ounce (7 milliliters); extra aged rum, 0.25 ounce (7 milliliters).

How to mix it: Carefully pour the beverages in each glass in the order they appear in the recipe, using a teaspoon to prevent them from blending. Pour part of the rum in a spoon and heat it with a match or a small burner until it flares. Pour it over the glass'rim.

The glass must be left to cool for a few seconds before drinking from it.

Dim the bar's lights to render the preparation of this cocktail more spectacular.

ARENAS DE ORO (GOLDEN SANDS)

Betweentimes cocktail, mixed in a cocktail shaker.

Serve it in a chilled, tall cocktail glass.

Ingredients: Refined sugar, 0.25 ounce (7 grams); lemon juice, 0.25 ounce (7 milliliters); grenadine, 5 drops; orange juice, 1.5 ounce (45 milliliters); old gold rum, 1.5 ounce (45 milliliters); ice cubes, 6 ounces (180 grams); the rind of 1 lemon or 1 orange peeled in a spiral.

How to mix it: Pour the sugar, the lemon juice and the grenadine drops into the cocktail shaker. Move the shaker circularly until the sugar dissolves. Add the remaining ingredients and shake for 15 seconds. Strain the mixture in the glass and garnish it with the spiral of orange or lemon rind.

Avispa (Wasp)

Hot cocktail, mixed in the serving glass.

Serve it in a thick, Old Fashion glass.

Ingredients: Refined sugar, 0.5 ounce (15 grams); hot fresh milk, 3 ounces (90 milliliters); light dry rum, 1.5 ounce (45 milliliters); 2 cloves.

How to mix it: Pour all the ingredients in the glass and stir.

Babalú

Fancy, betweentimes cocktail, prepared in an electric mixer.

Serve it in a 14-ounce glass.

Ingredients: Syrup, 1 ounce (30 milliliters); grapefruit juice, 2 ounces (60 milliliters); old gold rum, 2 ounces (60 milliliters); ice cubes, 5 ounces (150 grams); 1 peppermint sprig; 1 slice or "crescent" of orange; 1 slice of pineapple.

How to mix it: Pour the syrup, the grapefruit juice and the rum into the mixer and blend them. Place the ice in the serving glass and pour the mixture over it. Garnish it with the sprig of peppermint and the fruit slices. Serve it with a straw.

BANDERA TRICOLOR (THREE-COLORED FLAG)

Digestive cocktail stirred in the serving glass.

Serve it in a tall, 1.5-ounce cordial glass.

Ingredients: Grenadine, 0.5 ounce (15 milliliters); triple sec liquor, 0.5 ounce (15 milliliters); extra aged rum, 0.5 ounce (15 milliliters).

How to mix it: Carefully pour the beverages into the glass with a teaspoon so that they do not blend. They must be poured in the same order listed in the recipe.

BARACOA ESPECIAL (BARACOA SPECIAL)

Betweentimes cocktail prepared in an electric mixer.

Serve it in a chilled Daiquiri glass.

Ingredients: Lemon juice, 0.5 ounce (15 milliliters); coconut liquor, 0.15 ounce (5 milliliters); grapefruit juice, 1 ounce (30 milliliters); light dry rum, 1 ounce (30 milliliters); extra aged rum, 1 ounce (30 milliliters); frappé ice, 4 ounces (120 grams).

How to mix it: Pour all the ingredients—including the ice—in the mixer, and mix for 15 seconds. Serve it with a straw.

BELLOMONTE

Fancy, betweentimes cocktail, prepared in an electric mixer.

Serve it in a chilled, 8-ounce water glass.

Ingredients: Grenadine, 7 drops; cacao liquor, 10 drops; 1 round of lemon; refined sugar, 0.25 ounce (7 grams); lemon juice, 0.25 ounce (7 milliliters); maraschino, 5 drops; light dry rum, 1.5 ounce (45 milliliters); frappé ice, 4 ounces (120 grams); 1 sour red cherry; 1 sprig of peppermint; crême de menthe, 0.2 ounce (6 milliliters).

How to mix it: Pour the grenadine drops and the cacao liquor into the serving glass and cover them with the lemon round. Pour the sugar and the lemon juice into the mixer and move it circularly by hand until the sugar dissolves. Add the maraschino, the rum and the ice, and mix for 15 seconds. Carefully pour the mixture into the glass. Garnish it with the sour cherry and the peppermint sprig, and top it with the crême de menthe. Serve it with a straw.

BESO (KISS)

Digestive cocktail, stirred in the serving glass.

Serve it in a tall, 1.5-ounce cordial glass.

Ingredients: Triple sec liquor, 1 ounce (30 milliliters); milk cream, 0.5 ounce (15 milliliters); 1 red sour cherry.

How to mix it: Carefully pour the liquor and the cream (in that order) with a spoon into the cordial glass to prevent them from blending. Spear the sour cherry with a toothpick and top the cocktail with it, leaning the toothpick on the rim of the glass.

BOLA ROJA (RED BALL)

Apéritif stirred in the serving glass.

Serve it in a thick, Old Fashion glass.

Ingredients: Grenadine, 5 drops; lemon juice, 0.25 ounce (7 milliliters); light dry rum, 1.5 ounce (45 milliliters); ice cubes, 3 ounces (90 grams); 1 sprig of mint.

How to mix it: Pour all the ingredients into the glass and stir. Garnish it with the sprig of peppermint.

BRUJA BLANCA (WHITE WITCH)

Fancy, betweentimes cocktail, mixed in a cocktail shaker.

Serve it in an 8-ounce or a 10-ounce water glass.

Ingredients: Frappé ice, 4 ounces (120 grams); chocolate liquor, 0.25 ounce (7 milliliters); lemon juice, 0.25 ounce (7 milliliters); triple sec liquor, 0.25 ounce (7 milliliters); light dry rum, 1 ounce (30 milliliters); 1 slice of pineapple, 1 orange "crescent" and 1 sprig of peppermint.

How to mix it: Place the shaved ice in the serving glass. Pour the remaining ingredients in the shaker, and shake for 15 seconds. Pour the mixture over the ice. Garnish it with the slices of fruit and the sprig of peppermint. Serve it with a straw.

BUENAS NOCHES (GOOD NIGHT)

Nutritive cocktail, mixed in a cocktail shaker.

Serve it in a chilled, 6-ounce wine glass.

Ingredients: Refined sugar, 0.5 ounce (15 grams); 1 egg; cacao liquor, 0.5 ounce (15 milliliters); extra aged rum, 1.5 ounce (45 milliliters); ice cubes, 6 ounces (180 grams); ground nutmeg.

How to mix it: Pour the ingredients in the shaker, and shake for 15 seconds. Strain the mixture directly into the serving glass and sprinkle the ground nutmeg over it. Serve it with a straw.

CABALLITO (LITTLE PONY)

Apéritif mixed in a cocktail shaker.

Serve it in a tall cocktail glass.

Ingredients: A pinch of refined sugar; peppermint, 3 leaves; lemon juice, 0.25 ounce (7 milliliters); red vermouth, 0.5 ounce (15 milliliters); light dry rum, 1.5 ounces (45 milliliters); ice cubes, 6 ounces (180 grams).

How to mix it: Put the sugar and the peppermint leaves in the shaker. Bruise the leaves slightly with a spiral handle spoon. Add the lemon juice and stir in a circular motion to dissolve the sugar. Add the rest of the ingredients and shake for 15 seconds.

CACIQUE (CHIEFTAIN)

Refreshing cocktail stirred in the serving glass.

Serve it in a 10-ounce glass.

Ingredients: Dry anisette, 5 drops; syrup, 0.5 ounce (15 milliliters); lemon juice, 0.5 ounce (15 milliliters); light dry rum, 1.5 ounce (15 milliliters); cracked ice, 4 ounces (120 grams); soda water, 3 ounces (90 milliliters); 1 slice of lemon.

How to mix it: Pour all the ingredients into the serving glass and stir. Garnish the cocktail with the lemon slice. Serve it with a teaspoon and a straw.

CANCHÁNCHARA

Betweentimes cocktail stirred in the serving glass, coconut or gourd. (Although it can be served in a
6-ounce glass, the original cocktail is prepared and served
in a dry coconut shell or in a gourd, the fruit of the
calabash tree —*Crescentia cujete*, of the genus Bignonia—
that grows everywhere on the island.)

Ingredients: Honey, 0.5 ounce (15 milliliters); lemon
   juice, 0.5 ounce (15 milliliters); raw rum, 1.5 ounce
   (45 milliliters); water, 1 ounce (30 milliliters); cracked
   ice, 2 ounces (60 grams).

How to mix it: Pour the honey and the lemon juice
   into the container. Stir until the honey has dissolved.
   Add the raw rum, the ice and the water. Stir.

CARIBEÑO (CARIBBEAN)

Refreshing cocktail mixed in the serving glass.

Serve it in a 10-ounce glass.

Ingredients: Ice cubes, 4 ounces (120 grams); sugar,
   0.5 ounce (15 grams); lemon juice, 0.25 ounce
   (7 milliliters); coconut water, 3 ounces (90 milliliters); gin, 1.5 ounce (45 milliliters); 1 round of lemon.

How to mix it: Pour the ingredients in the serving glass
   and stir. Garnish it with the lemon round and serve
   it with a straw.

COCTEL CUBANO (CUBAN COCKTAIL)

Betweentimes cocktail mixed in a cocktail shaker.

Serve it in a shallow cocktail glass.

Ingredients: Refined sugar, 0.25 ounce (7 grams); lemon juice, 0.25 ounce (7 milliliters); light dry rum, 1.5 ounce (45 milliliters).

How to mix it: Place the sugar and the lemon juice in the shaker and move it circularly until the sugar is dissolved. Add the rum and shake for 15 seconds.

No ice is used in preparing this cocktail, served at room temperature.

COCTEL INFANTIL (COCKTAIL FOR CHILDREN)

Refreshing, non-alcoholic cocktail mixed in the serving glass.

Serve it in a 12-ounce glass.

Ingredients: Frappé ice: 6 ounces (180 grams); fruit juice, 3 ounces (90 milliliters); grenadine, 0.5 ounce (15 milliliters). One slice of pineapple, 1 orange "crescent" and 1 red sour cherry.

How to mix it: Pour the frappé ice, the lemon juice and the grenadine drops into the glass, and stir to blend them. Garnish the glass with the fruit slices, and serve it with a straw.

This cocktail was created for children and teetotallers.

COLONIAL

Apéritif prepared in the serving glass.

Serve it in an Old Fashion glass.

Ingredients: Angostura bitter, 5 drops; Amer Picon bitter, 5 drops; red curaçao, 5 drops; red vermouth,

2 ounces (60 milliliters); cracked ice, 3 ounces (90 grams); 1 strip of lemon rind and 1 sprig of peppermint.

How to mix it: Pour the ingredients in the glass and stir. Aromatize them with the lemon rind, expressing it over the top and adding it to the cocktail. Garnish it with the sprig of peppermint.

This cocktail was the hallmark of El Colonial, on Prado Avenue, one of the oldest and most exclusive restaurants in Havana.

XIII CONGRESO (13TH CONGRESS)

Betweentimes cocktail prepared in the serving glass.

Serve it in an Old Fashion glass.

Ingredients: A pinch of refined sugar; lemon juice, 4 drops; pineapple liquor, 0.25 ounce (7 milliliters); dry gin, 0.25 ounce (7 milliliters); old gold rum, 1.5 ounce (45 milliliters); cracked ice, 2 ounces (60 grams); 1 slice of pineapple; 1 orange "crescent"; 1 red sour cherry; 1 sprig of peppermint; red vermouth to sprinkle over the mixture, 0.25 ounces (7 milliliters).

How to mix it: Pour the sugar and the lemon juice in the serving glass and stir until the sugar dissolves. Add the rest of the ingredients and stir again. Garnish it with the fruit slices and the sprig of peppermint. Sprinkle with vermouth and serve it with straws.

This cocktail won the contest held on the occasion of the 13th Congress of the Cuban workers.

Contacto (Contact)

Apéritif mixed in a mixing glass.

Serve it in an Old Fashion glass.

Ingredients: Grenadine, 0.25 ounce (7 milliliters); cracked ice, 3 ounces (90 grams); orange juice, 0.25 ounce (7 milliliters); red vermouth, 0.25 ounce (7 milliliters); light dry rum, 1 ounce (30 milliliters); ice cubes, 3 ounces (90 grams); 1 red sour cherry; 1 orange "crescent".

How to mix it: Pour the grenadine with the cracked ice in the Old Fashion glass. Pour the remaining ingredients into the mixing glass. Stir for 10 seconds and strain them directly into the serving glass. Place the sour cherry in the glass and the orange "crescent" on its rim. Serve it with straws.

This cocktail was named after and dedicated to a famous Cuban TV show.

Costa Sur (South Coast)

Apéritif prepared in the serving glass.

Serve it in an Old Fashion glass.

Ingredients: Angostura bitter, 3 drops; peppermint, 1 sprig; pineapple liquor, 0.25 ounce (7 milliliters); light dry rum, 1.5 ounce (45 milliliters); cracked ice, 3 ounces (90 grams); 1 orange "crescent"; 1 strip of lemon rind.

How to mix it: Pour the angostura drops into the glass, add the sprig of peppermint and bruise it with the tip of a teaspoon. Add the rest of the ingredients and stir. Garnish it with the orange "crescent" and express the lemon rind over the top to aromatize the drink. Serve it with straws.

This cocktail is the hallmark of the Costa Sur Hotel, in the city of Trinidad.

CUBA BELLA (BEAUTIFUL CUBA)

Fancy, betweentimes cocktail, mixed in a cocktail shaker.

Serve it in an 8-ounce water glass.

Ingredients: Green crême de menthe, 0.25 ounce (7 milliliters); cracked ice, 4 ounces (120 grams); lemon juice, 0.25 ounce (7 milliliters); grenadine, 0.25 ounce (7 milliliters); light dry rum, 1.5 ounces (45 milliliters); ice cubes, 6 ounces (180 grams); extra aged rum, 0.25 ounce (7 milliliters); 1 orange "crescent"; 1 red sour cherry; 1 sprig of peppermint.

How to mix it: Carefully pour the crême de menthe into the serving glass so that it settles on the bottom. Cover it with the cracked ice. Add the lemon juice, the grenadine, the light dry rum and the ice cubes into the shaker. Shake for 15 seconds. Strain the mixture into the serving glass and garnish it with the fruit slices and the sprig of peppermint. Sprinkle the extra aged rum over the top. Serve it with straws.

The Cuba Bella cocktail won the first prize in a contest held in the 1960s.

CUBA LIBRE

Refreshing cocktail mixed in the serving glass.
Serve it in an 8-ounce glass.

Ingredients: Ice cubes, 3 ounces (30 grams); light dry rum, 1.5 ounces (45 milliliters); cola soda; a few drops of lemon juice; 1 round of lemon or 1 slice of lemon.

How to mix it: Put the ice in the glass, pour the rum over it and fill the rest with the cola soda. The lemon can be served either by adding a few drops to the cocktail, by placing a round on the rim of the glass, or by placing a slice on a small plate with the cocktail so that the drinker expresses the juice into the drink, to taste. Serve it with a stirrer.

"Viva Cuba Libre" (Long Live Free Cuba) was the war cry of the *mambises*—the combatants of the independence army—who fought to free Cuba from the Spanish colonial yoke in the wars of independence waged from 1868 to 1878 and from 1885 to 1898. Cuba Libre was one of the first cocktails to be mixed by Cuban bartenders. Despite the fact—or perhaps due to it—that it is a simple formula, it has attained worldwide fame.

CUBANITO

Apéritif prepared in the serving glass.

Serve it in an 8-ounce glass.

Ingredients: Lemon juice, 0.25 ounce (7 milliliters); a pinch of salt; Worcester sauce, 3 drops; hot sauce, 1 drop; tomato juice, 3 ounces (90 milliliters), light dry rum, 1.5 ounce (45 milliliters); cracked ice, 3 ounces (90 grams).

How to mix it: Pour all the ingredients in the serving glass and stir. Place a teaspoon in the glass. It can be garnished with a round of lemon.

CUBATABACO

Betweentimes cocktail mixed in the serving glass.

Serve it in a 6-ounce glass.

Ingredients: Cracked ice, 3 ounces (90 grams); cacao liquor, 1 ounce (30 milliliters); light dry rum, 1 ounce (30 milliliters); blue vegetal dye; 1 red sour cherry.

How to mix it: Pour the ice in the glass and cover it with the cacao liquor. Moist the tip of a toothpick and dip it in the blue dye, so only one drop sticks to it. Color the rum with the dye and pour it over the cacao liquor with a spoon to prevent them from blending. Spear the sour cherry with a toothpick and place it on top of the mixture, while resting the toothpick on the rim of the glass. Serve it with straws.

CUBATABACO is also the name of the export enterprise in charge of commercializing the superb Havana cigars.

CHAPARRA

Apéritif stirred in a mixing glass.

Serve it in a chilled, shallow cocktail glass.

Ingredients: Red vermouth, 0.5 ounce (15 milliliters); light dry rum, 1.25 ounce (37 milliliters); cracked ice; 6 ounces (180 grams); lemon rind.

How to mix it: Pour the ingredients into the mixing glass and stir for 10 seconds. Strain the mixture in the glass. Aromatize with the lemon rind, twisting it over the mixture and placing it inside the cocktail.

This is an old Cuban cocktail, dedicated to the famous Chaparra sugar mill.

CHICLET'S

Betweentimes cocktail prepared in an electric mixer.

Serve it in a chilled Daiquiri glass.

Ingredients: Refined sugar, 0.25 ounce (7 grams); lemon juice, 0.25 ounce (7 milliliters); grenadine, 5 drops; banana liquor, 0.5 ounce (15 milliliters), crême de menthe, 0.5 ounce (15 milliliters); light dry rum, 0.5 ounce (15 milliliters); frappé ice, 4 ounces (120 grams).

How to mix it: Put the sugar and the lemon juice in the mixer and dissolve the sugar by hand moving the mixer with a circular motion. Add the remaining ingredients. Blend them for 15 seconds. Pour the mixture in the glass and serve it with straws.

DAIQUIRÍ FRAPPÉ

Betweentimes cocktail prepared in an electric mixer.

Serve it in a chilled Daiquiri glass.

Ingredients: Maraschino, 5 drops; refined sugar, 0.25 ounce (7 grams); lemon juice, 0.25 ounce (7 milliliters); light dry rum, 1.5 ounce (45 milliliters); frappé ice, 4 ounces (120 grams).

How to mix it: Pour the maraschino drops, the sugar and the lemon juice in the mixer and dissolve the sugar moving the mixer's glass circularly by hand. Add the remaining ingredients and blend for 15 seconds. Serve it with straws.

This cocktail was created at the Daiquiri mines, located in Cuba's easternmost region, by an engineer who suffered from the intense heat that characterizes the area. Years later—in 1920—it was improved by Constantino Ribalaigua, known as Constante, the famous bartender at the Floridita bar in Havana. This is the exquisite and worldwide famous cocktail that Hemingway always drank at the Floridita, which he described in his novel *Islands in the Stream*.

Daiquirí Natural (Daiquiri au Naturel)

Apéritif mixed in a cocktail shaker.

Serve it in a chilled Daiquiri glass.

Ingredients: Maraschino, 5 drops; refined sugar, 0.25 ounce (7 grams); lemon juice, 0.25 ounce (7 milliliters); light dry rum, 1.5 ounce (45 milliliters); cracked ice, 6 ounces (180 grams).

How to mix it: Pour the maraschino, the sugar and the lemon juice in the shaker and move it circularly until the sugar dissolves. Add the rum and the cracked ice, and mix for 15 seconds. Strain it directly into the glass.

This is not a frappé cocktail, so it is considered an apéritif.

Daiquirí de Plátano (Banana Daiquiri)

Betweentimes cocktail prepared in an electric mixer.

Serve it in a chilled Daiquiri glass.

Ingredients: A pinch of refined sugar; lemon juice, 0.25 ounce (7 milliliters); light dry rum, 0.5 ounce (15 milliliters); banana liquor, 1 ounce (30 milliliters); frappé ice, 4 ounces (120 grams).

How to mix it. Pour the lemon juice and the sugar into the mixer, and move it circularly by hand until the sugar dissolves. Add the remaining ingredients and blend for 15 seconds. Serve it with straws.

DAIQUIRÍ DE PIÑA (PINEAPPLE DAIQUIRI)

Betweentimes cocktail prepared in an electric mixer.

Serve it in a chilled Daiquiri glass.

Ingredients: A pinch of refined sugar; lemon juice, 0.25 ounce (7 milliliters); light dry rum, 0.5 ounce (15 milliliters); pineapple liquor, 1 ounce (30 milliliters); frappé ice, 4 ounces (120 grams).

How to mix it: Pour the lemon juice and the sugar into the mixer and move it circularly by hand until the sugar dissolves. Add the remaining ingredients and blend for 15 seconds. Serve it with straws.

DAIQUIRÍ REBELDE (REBEL DAIQUIRI)

Betweentimes cocktail prepared in an electric mixer.

Serve it in a chilled Daiquiri glass.

Ingredients: A pinch of refined sugar; lemon juice, 0.25 ounce (7 milliliters); green crême de menthe, 0.25 ounce (7 milliliters); light dry rum, 1.5 ounce (45 milliliters); frappé ice, 4 ounces (120 grams).

How to mix it: Pour the lemon juice and the sugar into the mixer, and move it circularly by hand until the sugar dissolves. Add the remaining ingredients and blend for 15 seconds. Serve it with straws.

Rebel Daiquiri takes its name after the cocktail's olive-green hue, which is the color of the Cuban Armed Forces' uniform. It was created in 1959, after the triumph of the Revolution.

ENROQUE (CASTLING)

Fancy apéritif, stirred in a mixing glass.

Serve it in an 8-ounce water glass.

Ingredients: Cracked ice, 4 ounces (120 grams); angostura bitter, 5 drops; triple sec liquor, 0.25 ounce (7 milliliters); red vermouth, 0.5 ounce (15 milliliters); old gold rum, 1.5 ounce (45 milliliters); ice cubes, 6 ounces (180 grams). The rind of 1 orange peeled as a spiral.

How to mix it: Put the ice in the serving glass. Pour the remaining ingredients in the mixing glass and stir for 10 seconds. Strain them into the serving glass and garnish it with the orange rind, imitating a horse's neck. Serve it with straws.

This cocktail was created on the occasion of the Capablanca In Memoriam Chess Tournaments, held in Cuba for many years since the 1960s.

ERNEST HEMINGWAY ESPECIAL (ERNEST HEMINGWAY SPECIAL)

Betweentimes cocktail prepared in an electric mixer.

Serve it in a chilled Daiquiri glass.

Ingredients: Maraschino, 0.25 ounce (7 milliliters); lemon juice, 0.25 ounce (7 milliliters); grapefruit juice,

0.25 ounce (7 milliliters); light dry rum, 2 ounces (60 milliliters); frappé ice, 4 ounces (120 grams).

How to mix it: Pour all the ingredients into the mixer and blend for 15 seconds. Pour the mixture in the glass and serve it with straws.

This cocktail has no sugar. That is how the famous writer liked to drink it at the Floridita restaurant's bar.

ENSALADA DE FRUTAS (FRUIT SALAD)

Refreshing cocktail mixed in the serving glass.

Serve it in a 12-ounce glass.

Ingredients: Frappé ice, 3 ounces (90 grams); grenadine, 0.25 ounce (7 milliliters); various fruits cut into small cubes, 3 ounces (90 grams) [the fruits more often used for this cocktail in Cuba are pineapple, orange, grapefruit and sour cherries, but they can be replaced by others]; lemon soda, 3 ounces (90 milliliters).

How to mix it: Pour all the ingredients in the glass and stir slightly. Serve it with a spoon and straws.

This cocktail is welcomed by teetotallers on hot summer afternoons.

ESPERANZA (HOPE)

Refreshing cocktail mixed in the serving glass.

Serve it in a 10-ounce glass

Ingredients: Syrup, 0.5 ounce (15 milliliters); lemon juice, 0.5 ounce (15 milliliters); crême de menthe, 5 drops; light dry rum, 1.5 ounce (45 milliliters);

cracked ice, 4 ounces (120 grams); soda water, 3 ounces (90 milliliters); 1 round of lemon.

How to mix it: Pour all the ingredients in the glass and stir. Garnish it with the round of lemon, placed on the rim of the glass. Serve it with straws.

FLAMENCO

Fancy, betweentimes cocktail, mixed in a cocktail shaker.

Serve it in an 8-ounce water glass.

Ingredients: Grenadine, a dash; cracked ice, 4 ounces (120 grams); refined sugar, 0.25 ounce (7 grams); lemon juice, 0.25 ounce (7 milliliters); light dry rum, 1 ounce (30 milliliters); ice cubes, 6 ounces (180 grams); extra aged rum, 1 ounce (30 milliliters); Amer Picon, 3 drops; 1 slice of pineapple; 1 red sour cherry; 1 sprig of peppermint.

How to mix it: Put the grenadine on the bottom of the glass and add the cracked ice. Pour the lemon juice and the sugar into the shaker and dissolve the sugar with a circular motion. Add the light dry rum and the ice cubes and shake for 15 seconds. Strain the mixture over the cracked ice in the glass. Garnish it with the fruit slices and the sprig of peppermint. Pour the extra aged rum and the Amer Picon over it.

In the 1960s, this cocktail was the hallmark of the famous Flamenco Bar at the Sevilla Hotel.

FLAMINGO

Betweentimes cocktail prepared in an electric mixer. Serve it in a chilled Daiquiri glass.

Ingredients: One dash of grenadine; lemon juice, 0.5 ounce (15 milliliters); syrup, 0.5 ounce (15 milliliters); pineapple juice, 0.5 ounce (15 milliliters); light dry rum, 1 ounce (30 milliliters); frappé ice, 4 ounces (120 grams).

How to mix it: Pour all the ingredients in the mixer and blend for 15 seconds. Serve it with straws.

This cocktail represented the Flamingo Hotel in Havana.

FLORIDITA ESPECIAL (FLORIDITA SPECIAL)

Betweentimes cocktail mixed in a cocktail shaker.

Serve it in a chilled, shallow cocktail glass.

Ingredients: Red curaçao, 10 drops; maraschino, 10 drops; orange juice, 0.5 ounce (15 milliliters); old gold rum, 1.5 ounce (45 milliliters); cracked ice, 6 ounces (180 grams).

How to mix it: Pour the ingredients in the shaker and blend them for 15 seconds. Strain them directly into the glass.

FOGATA (BONFIRE)

Hot cocktail, prepared in the serving glass.

Serve it in an Old Fashion glass.

Ingredients: Red curaçao, 0.5 ounce (15 milliliters); extra aged rum, 1.5 ounce (45 milliliters); hot water, 3 ounces (90 milliliters); 1 round of lemon.

How to mix it: Pour all the ingredients in the serving glass and stir.

GINEBRA COMPUESTA (GIN MIX)

Apéritif mixed in the serving glass.

Serve it in a 6-ounce glass.

Ingredients: Refined sugar: 0.25 ounce (7 grams; lemon juice, 0.25 ounce (7 milliliters); angostura bitter, 3 drops; dry gin, 1.5 ounce (45 milliliters); cracked ice, 2 ounces (60 grams); 1 round of lemon.

How to mix it: Pour the sugar and the lemon juice in the glass and stir with a teaspoon until the sugar is dissolved. Add the remaining ingredients and stir again. Garnish it with the round of lemon.

When ice was not yet manufactured in Cuba, this cocktail was very popular among cartdrivers, who drank it in the early morning. Currently, the flavor of angostura and the freshness of the "cooling stone", like someone once called ice, have turned this cocktail into a veritable delight.

HAVANA CLUB

Apéritif mixed in a cocktail shaker.

Serve it in a chilled, shallow cocktail glass.

Ingredients: Light dry Havana Club rum, 1 ounce (30 milliliters); dry vermouth, 0.5 ounce (15 milliliters); cracked ice, 6 ounces (180 grams); 1 red sour cherry.

How to mix it: Pour the ingredients in the cocktail shaker and shake for 15 seconds. Strain into the glass and top with the sour cherry.

HAVANA ESPECIAL (HAVANA SPECIAL)

Betweentimes cocktail, mixed in a cocktail shaker.

Serve it in a chilled, 6-ounce glass.

Ingredients: Maraschino, 0.2 ounce (6 milliliters); pine-apple juice, 1.5 ounce (45 milliliters); light dry rum, 1.5 ounce (45 milliliters); cracked ice, 6 ounces (180 grams).

How to mix it: Put the ingredients in the shaker and blend them for 15 seconds. Put an ice cube in the glass and strain the mixture over it.

HAVANA ROCA (HAVANA ROCK)

Betweentimes cocktail, stirred in the serving glass.

Serve it in an Old Fashion glass.

Ingredients: Lemon juice, 0.5 ounce (15 milliliters); grenadine, 0.5 ounce (15 milliliters); dry white vermouth, 0.25 ounce (7 milliliters); triple sec liquor, 0.5 ounce (15 milliliters); dry gin, 1.5 ounce (45 milliliters); cracked ice, 3 ounces (90 grams); 1 orange "crescent", 1 round of lemon, 1 sprig of peppermint.

How to mix it: Pour all the ingredients into the serving glass and stir. Garnish it with the fruit and the sprig of peppermint. Serve it with straws.

This cocktail was specially created for the restaurant La Roca (The Rock), in Havana.

HASTA LUEGO (SO LONG)

Nutritive cocktail mixed in a cocktail shaker.

Serve it in a chilled, 10-ounce glass.

Ingredients: Refined sugar, 0.5 ounce (15 grams); fresh milk, 3 ounces (90 milliliters); 1 egg; cacao liquor, 0.5 ounce (15 milliliters); light dry rum, 1.5 ounce (45 milliliters); cracked ice, 6 ounces (180 grams); ground nutmeg.

How to mix it: Pour the milk and the sugar into the cocktail shaker and move it circularly until the sugar dissolves. Add the remaining ingredients and shake for 15 seconds. Strain the mixture into the glass and sprinkle it with the ground nutmeg.

IDEAL

Apéritif mixed in a cocktail shaker.

Serve it in a chilled, tall cocktail glass.

Ingredients: Maraschino, 10 drops; grapefruit juice, 0.5 ounce (15 milliliters); red vermouth, 0.5 ounce (15 milliliters); dry white vermouth, 0.5 ounce (15 milliliters); dry gin, 1 ounce (30 milliliters); cracked ice, 6 ounces (180 grams); 1 roast almond.

How to mix it: Pour all the ingredients into the cocktail mixer and shake them for 15 seconds. Strain the mixture into the glass and garnish it with the roast almond.

This cocktail was very popular in restaurants' bars in the 1950s.

ISLA AZUL (BLUE ISLAND)

Fancy, betweentimes cocktail mixed in a cocktail shaker.

Serve it in a 10-ounce water glass.

Ingredients: Pineapple liquor, 0.25 ounce (7 milliliters); cracked ice, 4 ounces (120 grams); lemon juice, 0.25 ounce (7 milliliters); crême de menthe, 0.5 ounce (15 milliliters); light dry rum, 1.5 ounce (45 milliliters); blue curaçao, 0.25 ounce (7 milliliters); 1 sprig of peppermint; 1 round of pineapple shaped like a sun; 1 red sour cherry.

How to mix it: Pour the pineapple liquor into the glass and cover it with the cracked ice. Pour the lemon juice, the crême de menthe and the rum into the shaker and mix for 10 seconds. Pour the mixture into the glass and sprinkle it with the blue curaçao. Place the pineapple sun on the rim of the glass, and garnish it with the sprig of peppermint and the red sour cherry. Serve it with straws.

ISLA DE PINOS (ISLE OF PINES)

Apéritif prepared in a cocktail shaker.

Serve it in a chilled, shallow cocktail glass.

Ingredients: Refined sugar, 0.25 ounce (7 grams); grapefruit juice, 0.5 ounce (15 milliliters); red vermouth, 0.5 ounce (15 milliliters); light dry rum, 1 ounce (30 milliliters); cracked ice, 6 ounces (180 grams).

How to mix it: Dissolve the sugar in the grapefruit juice in the shaker. Add the vermouth, the rum and the ice and shake for 15 seconds. Strain into the glass. Garnish it to taste.

The Isle of Pines is currently called Isle of Youth. It is said it was the island that inspired Robert Louis Stevenson to write his novel *Treasure Island*.

Jai Alai

Apéritif prepared in the serving glass.

Serve it in an 8-ounce glass.

Ingredients: Refined sugar, 0.25 ounce (7 grams); lemon juice, 0.25 ounce (7 milliliters); red vermouth, 0.5 ounce (15 milliliters); dry gin, 1 ounce (30 milliliters); cracked ice, 3 ounces (90 grams); soda water, 3 ounces (90 milliliters).

How to mix it: Pour all the ingredients in the serving glass and stir slightly.

This cocktail was very popular among professional jai alai players since colonial times.

Limonada Clarete (Claret Lemonade)

Refreshing cocktail mixed in the serving glass.

Serve it in a 14-ounce glass.

Ingredients: Refined sugar, 0.5 ounce (15 grams); lemon juice, 2 ounces (60 milliliters); water, 4 ounces (120 milliliters); red wine, 2 ounces (60 milliliters); cracked ice, 3 ounces (90 grams); 1 round of lemon.

How to mix it: Pour the lemon juice, the water, the sugar and the ice in the serving glass and stir. Carefully add the wine to prevent it from blending with the other ingredients. Place the lemon slice on the glass' rim. Serve it with straws.

Lobo de Mar (Old Salt)

Apéritif prepared in a mixing glass.
Serve it in a chilled, shallow cocktail glass.

Ingredients: Red curaçao, 5 drops; dry sherry, 0.5 ounce (15 milliliters); light dry rum, 1.5 ounce (45 milliliters); cracked ice, 6 ounces (180 grams).

How to mix it: Pour the ingredients into the mixing glass and stir for 15 seconds. Strain the mixture into the glass.

MARY PICKFORD

Betweentimes cocktail, prepared in an electric mixer.

Serve it in a chilled, tall cocktail glass.

Ingredients: Grenadine, 0.15 milliliters; pineapple juice, 1.5 ounce (45 milliliters); light dry rum, 1.5 ounce (45 milliliters); cracked ice, 6 ounces (180 grams).

How to mix it: Pour the ingredients into the mixer and shake for 15 seconds. Strain the mixture into the glass.

Although this cocktail was named after the famous North American actress, it was created in Cuba.

MOJITO

Apéritif mixed in the serving glass.

Serve it in an 8-ounce glass.

Ingredients: One sprig of peppermint; refined sugar, 0.25 ounce (7 grams); lemon juice, 0.25 ounce (7 milliliters); light dry rum, 1.5 ounce (45 milliliters); soda water, 3 ounces (90 milliliters); cracked ice, 3 ounces (90 grams); angostura bitter, 3 drops.

How to mix it: Put the sugar, the lemon juice and the peppermint sprig in the glass, and bruise the peppermint leaves with the tip of a spoon. Add part of the water to dissolve the sugar. Add the rum, the ice, the drops of angostura and the rest of the water, and stir.

A more simple variant of this recipe leaves out the angostura drops and uses the sprig of peppermint like decoration. In this case, the cocktail is served with a spoon the drinker can use to bruise the peppermint leaves himself.

This cocktail, together with the Cuba Libre and the Daiquiri, ranks among the most famous Cuban cocktails. It is a very popular drink among the patrons and visitors of Havana's restaurant La Bodeguita del Medio.

MULATA

Betweentimes cocktail prepared in an electric mixer.

Serve it in a chilled Daiquiri glass.

Ingredients: Refined sugar, 0.15 ounce (5 grams); lemon juice, 0.25 ounce (7 milliliters); cacao liquor, 0.5 ounce (15 milliliters); extra aged rum, 1 ounce (30 milliliters); frappé ice, 4 ounces (120 grams).

How to mix it: Pour the lemon juice and the sugar into the mixer's glass and move it circularly until the sugar dissolves. Add the remaining ingredients and blend for 15 seconds. Serve it with straws.

NIÑA BONITA

Nutritive cocktail, prepared in a cocktail shaker.
Serve it in a chilled, 10-ounce glass.

Ingredients: Refined sugar, 0.5 ounce (15 grams); fresh milk, 3 ounces (90 milliliters); grenadine, 0.5 ounce (15 milliliters); extra aged rum, 0.5 ounce (15 milliliters); light dry rum, 1.5 ounce (45 milliliters); ice cubes, 6 ounces (180 grams); ground nutmeg.

How to mix it: Pour the milk and the sugar into the shaker and move it circularly until the sugar dissolves. Add the remaining ingredients and shake for 15 seconds. Strain the mixture into the glass and sprinkle it with the ground nutmeg.

Niña Bonita is the name of a well known cattle breeding center in Cuba.

NUBE ROSADA (PINK CLOUD)

Betweentimes cocktail mixed in a cocktail shaker.

Serve it in a chilled 6-ounce wine glass.

Ingredients: Grenadine, 5 drops; pineapple liquor, 0.25 ounce (7 milliliters); chocolate liquor, 0.5 ounce (15 milliliters); milk cream, 1 ounce (30 milliliters); extra aged rum, 1 ounce (30 milliliters); cracked ice, 6 ounces (180 grams); ground cinnamon.

How to mix it: Pour all the ingredients, except the ground cinnamon, into the cocktail shaker, and shake for 15 seconds. Strain the mixture directly into the glass and sprinkle it with the ground cinnamon. Serve it with straws.

OIP (INTERNATIONAL JOURNALISTS' ORGANIZATION)

Apéritif stirred in a mixing glass.

Serve it in a chilled 6-ounce wine glass.

Ingredients: Amaro Cinzano, 0.2 ounce (6 milliliters); sweet white vermouth, 1 ounce (30 milliliters); old gold rum, 1.5 ounce (45 milliliters); cracked ice, 3 ounces (90 grams); the rind of 1 lemon.

How to mix it: Pour the Cinzano, the white sweet vermouth and the rum in the mixing glass and stir. Put the ice in the glass and pour the mixture over it. Express the lemon rind over the cocktail, and put it in the glass. Serve it with straws.

This cocktail won the first prize in a contest held on the occasion of the Congress of the International Journalists' Organization held in Cuba in the 1960s.

Paloma Blanca (White Dove)

Digestive cocktail mixed in the serving glass.

Serve it in an 8-ounce glass.

Ingredients: Sweet or dry anisette, 1 ounce (30 milliliters); ice cubes, 3 ounces (90 grams); soda water, 3 ounces (90 milliliters).

How to mix it: Pour the ingredients in the serving glass and stir.

Pecho de Doncella (Maiden's Bosom)

Digestive cocktail mixed in the serving glass.

Serve it in a tall, 1.5-ounce cordial glass.

Ingredients: Cacao liquor, 1 ounce (30 milliliters); milk cream, 0.5 ounce (15 milliliters); 1 red sour cherry.

How to mix it: Carefully pour each of the beverages into the glass, using a spoon to prevent them from blending, in the same order they are mentioned in the recipe. Spear the sour cherry with a toothpick and place it near the rim of the glass.

PÉTALO (PETAL)

Betweentimes cocktail stirred in a mixing glass.

Serve it in a chilled, 2-ounce cordial glass.

Ingredients: Grenadine, 0.2 ounce (6 milliliters); anisette, 0.5 ounce (15 milliliters); dry white wine, 1 ounce (30 milliliters); ice cubes, 6 ounces (180 grams); 1 rose petal.

How to mix it: Pour the ingredients in the mixing glass and stir for 10 seconds. Strain the mixture in the serving glass and garnish it with the rose petal.

PINAREÑO

Digestive cocktail stirred in a mixing glass.

Serve it in a cocktail glass.

Ingredients: Crême de menthe, 0.5 ounce (15 milliliters); dry Guayabita del Pinar, 0.5 ounce (15 milliliters); light dry rum, 1 ounce (30 milliliters); ice cubes, 6 ounces (180 grams).

How to mix it: Pour the ingredients into the mixing glass and stir for 10 seconds. Strain the mixture into the serving glass.

Guayabita del Pinar is a liquor produced only in the westernmost Cuban province of Pinar del Río.

PINERITO

Apéritif mixed in a cocktail shaker.

Serve it in a chilled, tall cocktail glass.

Ingredients: Grenadine, 0.1 ounce (3 milliliters); grapefruit juice, 1.5 ounces (45 milliliters); light dry rum, 1.5 ounce (45 milliliters); ice cubes, 6 ounces (180 grams); the rind of 1 grapefruit.

How to mix it: Pour all the ingredients in the cocktail shaker and shake for 15 seconds. Strain the mixture into the glass, and aromatize with the grapefruit rind, twisting it over the glass before placing it inside the cocktail.

PONCHE DE FRUTAS (FRUIT PUNCH)

Refreshing cocktail, stirred in the serving glass.

Serve it in a 12-ounce glass.

Ingredients: Lemon juice, 0.25 ounce (7 milliliters); syrup, 1 ounce (30 milliliters); pineapple juice, 2 ounces (60 milliliters); grapefruit juice, 2 ounces (60 milliliters); frappé ice, 4 ounces (120 grams); 1 slice of pineapple; 1 orange "crescent"; 1 red sour cherry.

How to mix it: Pour the ingredients in the glass and stir. Add the frappé ice and garnish it with the fruits. Serve it with straws.

PRESIDENTE (PRESIDENT)

Apéritif stirred in a mixing glass.

Serve it in a chilled, shallow cocktail glass.

Ingredients: Red curaçao, 0.5 ounce (15 millilliters); sweet white vermouth, 0.5 ounce (15 milliliters); light dry rum, 1.5 ounce (45 milliliters); ice cubes, 6 ounces (180 grams); 1 red sour cherry; the rind of 1 orange.

How to mix it: Pour the ingredients in the mixing glass and stir for 10 seconds. Strain the mixture into the serving glass, top it with the sour cherry and aromatize it with the orange rind, twisting it over the mixture and placing it in the cocktail.

PRESIDENTE DULCE (SWEET PRESIDENT)

Apéritif stirred in a mixing glass.

Serve it in a chilled, shallow cocktail glass.

Ingredients: Red curaçao, 0.1 ounce (3 milliliters); grenadine, 0.1 ounce (3 milliliters); sweet white vermouth, 0.5 ounce (15 milliliters); light dry rum, 1.5 ounce (45 milliliters); cracked ice, 6 ounces (180 grams); 1 slice of orange rind, 1 red sour cherry.

How to mix it: Pour the ingredients in the mixing glass and stir for 10 seconds. Strain the mixture in the serving glass, top it with the sour cherry and aromatize it with the orange rind, twisting it over the cocktail. Drop the twisted orange rind into the cocktail.

PRESIDENTE SECO (DRY PRESIDENT)

Apéritif stirred in a mixing glass.

Serve it in a chilled, shallow cocktail glass.

Ingredients: Red curaçao, 0.15 ounce (5 milliliters); dry white vermouth, 0.5 ounce (15 milliliters); light dry rum, 1.5 ounce (45 milliliters); cracked ice, 6 ounces (180 grams); 1 olive, 1 slice of orange rind.

How to mix it: Pour the ingredients in the mixing glass and stir for 10 seconds. Place the olive in the serving glass and strain the mixture over it. Aromatize it with the orange rind, twisting it over the cocktail. Drop the twisted orange rind into the cocktail.

PRIMERO DE MAYO (FIRST OF MAY)

Betweentimes cocktail, stirred in a mixing glass.

Serve it in a chilled Daiquiri glass.

Ingredients: Grenadine, 0.1 ounce (3 milliliters); lemon juice, 0.2 ounce (6 milliliters); triple sec liquor, 0.5 ounce (15 milliliters); dry gin, 1.5 ounce (45 milliliters); cracked ice, 3 ounces (90 grams); 1 lemon round; 1 red sour cherry; 1 sprig of peppermint.

How to mix it: Pour the ingredients in the mixing glass and stir for 10 seconds. Strain the mixture into the serving glass. Place the lemon round on the rim of the glass. Top the cocktail with the sour cherry and the sprig of peppermint. Serve it with straws.

PUNCH DEAUVILLE

Fancy, betweentimes cocktail, mixed in a cocktail shaker.

Serve it in an 8-ounce water glass.

Ingredients: Refined sugar, 0.25 ounce (7 grams); lemon juice, 0.25 ounce (7 milliliters); pineapple juice, 0.5 ounce (15 milliliters); light dry rum, 1.5 ounce (45 milliliters); extra aged rum, 0.5 ounce (15 milliliters); ice cubes, 6 ounces (180 grams); cracked ice, 4 ounces (120 grams); 1 lemon round; 1 slice of pineapple; 1 sprig of peppermint.

How to mix it: Pour the pineapple juice and the lemon juice in the shaker together with the sugar, and move it in a circle to dissolve the sugar. Add the light dry rum and the ice cubes and shake for 15 seconds. Put the cracked ice in the serving glass and strain the mixture over it. Garnish it with the fruit slices and the sprig of peppermint. Pour the extra aged rum over the mixture carefully, to prevent it from blending with the cocktail. Serve it with straws.

This cocktail represents the famous Deauville Hotel, located on the Malecón, Havana's seaside drive.

RESCATE (RESCUE)

Hot cocktail stirred in a mixing glass.

Serve it in an Old Fashion glass.

Ingredients: Refined sugar, 1 ounce (30 grams); 1 egg yolk; hot milk, 4 ounces (120 milliliters); old gold rum, 2 ounces (60 milliliters).

How to mix it: Pour the egg yolk and the sugar into the mixing glass, and stir with a teaspoon to dissolve the sugar. Add the milk and the rum and stir again. Pour the liquid from one glass to another a few times to work up a light foam. Strain it into the serving glass.

Ron Achampañado (Champagne-like Rum)

Apéritif stirred in the serving glass.

Serve it in an 8-ounce glass.

Ingredients: Refined sugar, 0.25 ounce (7 grams); lemon juice, 0.25 ounce (7 milliliters); light dry rum, 1 ounce (30 milliliters); soda water, 3 ounces (90 milliliters); ice cubes, 3 ounces (90 grams).

How to mix it: Pour the lemon juice and the sugar into the glass and dissolve the sugar with a teaspoon. Add the ice and the rum. Fill the rest of the glass with soda water. Stir slightly and serve it with a small teaspoon.

Santiago

Betweentimes cocktail prepared in an electric mixer.

Serve it in a chilled Daiquiri glass.

Ingredients: Maraschino, 5 drops; lemon juice, 0.25 ounce (7 milliliters); grenadine, 0.5 ounce (15 milliliters); light dry rum, 1.5 ounce (45 milliliters); frappé ice, 4 ounces (120 grams).

How to mix it: Pour the ingredients in the mixer and blend for 15 seconds. Pour the mixture in the serving glass. Serve it with straws.

Saoco

Refreshing cocktail, stirred in a mixing glass.

Although it can be served in an 8-ounce glass, the way in which it was originally served is in the shell of a green coconut. The upper part of the coconut is cut off and a 4 cm hole is bored into it.

Ingredients: Light dry rum, 2 ounces (60 milliliters); coconut water; ice cubes, 6 ounces (180 grams).

How to mix it: Pour the ingredients in the mixing glass and stir for 10 seconds. Strain the mixture into the open coconut. Serve it with straws.

If a serving glass is used instead of a coconut shell, the rum and the ice cubes are put in it before filling it with coconut water.

This cocktail can also be mixed by previously chilling the coconut, opening it, pouring out some of its water, and adding the rum and stirring the mixture.

If a coconut shell is used to serve this cocktail, a teaspoon must be placed alongside it, so that the customer can also eat the coconut meat after drinking the cocktail.

SIERRA ORIENTAL (EASTERN SIERRA)

Fancy, betweentimes cocktail, prepared in a cocktail shaker.

Serve it in an 8-ounce water glass.

Ingredients: Syrup, 0.5 ounce (15 milliliters); lemon juice, 0.5 ounce (15 milliliters); orange juice, 1 ounce (30 milliliters); light dry rum, 1 ounce (30 milliliters), dry gin, 0.5 ounce (15 milliliters); brandy, 0.5 ounce (15 milliliters); ice cubes, 6 ounces (180 grams); cracked ice, 4 ounces (120 grams); lemon rounds; 1 orange "crescent".

How to mix it: Pour all the liquid ingredients and the ice cubes into the shaker. Shake for 15 seconds. Fill the serving glass with the cracked ice and strain the mixture over it. Garnish it with the fruit. Serve it with straws.

SOLDADOR (WELDER)

Hot cocktail stirred in the serving glass.

Serve it in an Old Fashion glass.

Ingredients: Refined sugar, 0.25 ounce (7 grams); hot tea, 3 ounces (90 milliliters); old gold rum, 1.5 ounce (45 milliliters); 1 round of lemon.

How to mix it: Pour the sugar and the tea into the serving glass. Stir to dissolve the sugar. Add the rum and stir again. Garnish it with the lemon round. Serve it with a small teaspoon.

SOL Y SOMBRA (SUNSHINE AND SHADOW)

Digestive cocktail mixed in the serving glass.

Serve it in a tall 1.5-ounce cordial glass.

Ingredients: Chocolate liquor, 1 ounce (30 milliliters); extra aged rum, 0.5 ounce (15 milliliters).

To mix it: Carefully pour the ingredients in the glass over a teaspoon to prevent them from blending, in the order in which they appear in the recipe.

TESORO (TREASURE)

Hot cocktail stirred in the serving glass.

Serve it in an Old Fashion glass.

Ingredients: Honey, 1.5 ounce (45 milliliters); hot tea, 3 ounces (90 milliliters); light dry rum, 2 ounces (60 milliliters).

How to mix it: Pour the honey and the tea in the glass. Stir to dissolve the honey. Add the rum and stir again.

Típico (Typical)

Digestive cocktail stirred in the serving glass.

Serve it in a 1.5-ounce cordial glass.

Ingredients:: Triple sec liquour, 1 ounce (30 milliliters); extra aged rum, 0.5 ounce (15 milliliters).

How to mix it: Carefully pour the ingredients in the glass, using a teaspoon to prevent them from blending, in the order in which they appear in the recipe.

Toronjil (Grapefruit Balm)

Refreshing cocktail stirred in the serving glass.

Serve it in an 8-ounce glass.

Ingredients: Dry gin, 1.5 ounce (45 milliliters); grapefruit juice, 3 ounces (90 milliliters); ice cubes.

How to mix it: Pour the ingredients in the glass and stir.

Tricontinental

Betweentimes cocktail stirred in the serving glass.

Serve it in a tall, champagne glass.

Ingredients: Lemon juice, 0.25 ounce (7 milliliters); grenadine, 0.15 ounce (5 milliliters); cacao liquor, 0.5 ounce (15 milliliters); old gold rum, 2 ounces (60 milliliters); cracked ice, 3 ounces (90 grams); 1 pineapple slice; 1 orange "crescent"; 1 red sour cherry; 1 sprig of peppermint.

How to mix it: Put the cracked ice in the glass and carefully pour the lemon juice, the grenadine, the cacao liquor and the old gold rum, so they do not mix. Garnish it with the fruit slices and the sprig of peppermint. Serve it with straws.

This cocktail won the prize awarded in a competition held in Cuba in the 1960s to choose the cocktail that would represent the gastronomy sector at the Tricontinental Conference, in which figures from Asia, Africa and Latin America participated.

TROPICAL

Betweentimes cocktail mixed in a cocktail shaker.

Serve it in a chilled, tall cocktail glass.

Ingredients: Grenadine, 2 drops; refined sugar, 0.25 ounce (7 grams); lemon juice, 0.5 ounce (15 milliliters); orange juice, 0.5 ounce (15 milliliters); 1 egg white; light dry rum, 1.5 ounces (45 milliliters); ice cubes, 6 ounces (180 grams).

How to mix it: Pour the grenadine, the fruit juices and the sugar into the shaker, and move it circularly until the sugar dissolves. Add the remaining ingredients and shake for 15 seconds. Frost the rim of the glass with sugar, and strain the cocktail in it.

TROPICANA ESPECIAL (TROPICANA SPECIAL)

Betweentimes cocktail prepared in an electric mixer.

Serve it in a chilled Daiquiri glass.

Ingredients: Refined sugar, 0.15 ounce (5 grams); lemon juice, 0.25 ounce (7 milliliters); maraschino, 5 drops; grenadine, 5 drops; light dry rum, 1.5 ounce (45 milliliters); frappé ice, 4 ounces (120 grams).

How to mix it: Dissolve the sugar in the mixer, moving it circularly by hand. Add the rest of the ingredients and blend for 15 seconds. Pour the mixture into the serving glass. Serve with it straws.

This cocktail was named after the famous Tropicana nightclub, also known as Paradise Under the Stars.

TURQUINO

Fancy, betweentimes cocktail, mixed in a cocktail shaker.

Serve it in a 12-ounce glass.

Ingredients: Grenadine, 0.2 ounce (6 milliliters); red curaçao, 0.5 ounce (15 milliliters); pineapple juice, 2 ounces (60 milliliters); light dry rum, 0.5 ounce (15 milliliters); extra aged rum, 1 ounce (30 milliliters); frappé ice, 5 ounces (145 grams); 1 sprig of peppermint.

How to mix it: Pour all liquid ingredients into the shaker and shake for 15 seconds. Fill the serving glass with frappé ice and pour the mixture over it. Garnish it with the sprig of peppermint. Serve it with straws.

This cocktail was named after the highest mountain in the Cuban archipelago. Turquino is in Cuba's easternmost region.

VARADERO (VARADERO BEACH)

Apéritif stirred in the serving glass.

Serve it in an Old Fashion glass.

Ingredients: Angostura bitter, 3 drops; refined sugar, 0.15 ounce (5 grams); lemon juice, 0.25 ounce (7 milliliters); old gold rum, 1.5 ounce (45 milliliters); cracked ice, 3 ounces (90 grams); 1 slice of pineapple; 1 orange "crescent"; 1 sprig of peppermint.

How to mix it: Pour the bitter drops, the sugar and the lemon juice into the glass. Stir to dissolve the sugar. Add the rum and the ice and stir again. Garnish it with the fruit and the sprig of peppermint. Serve with it straws.

Se terminó la impresión de esta obra,
en los talleres gráficos de
EDITORIAL LINOTIPIA BOLÍVAR
Y CÍA. S. EN C.,
de la Calle·10 No. 26-47, tel. 3600455,
en el mes de Julio de 2004.
Bogotá, D. C. - Colombia